GU00836350

STOIC QUOTES

365 Daily Reflections & Thoughts
of Wisdom to Strengthen your Perspective.

Tate Harris

Prologue

Stoicism is an ancient philosophy adopted by many in the pursuit of self-mastery, perseverance, and wisdom. Reading into the philosophy of Stoicism uncovers enlightening perspectives to cultivate one's mind.

Stoics recognize that every individual has a tendency to express destructive emotions. However, a shift in the way we think can help to overcome these undesirable sentiments, and develop a more healthy, and stable character that embodies a state of calm. It is a practical philosophy of personal ethics informed by a system of logic and its outlook on the natural world.

In the fore coming pages, you will explore a thought a day to help strengthen your perspective. If preferred, flick to a random page and indulge in numerous thought-provoking quotes anytime you are seeking clarity, perspective, or wisdom.

1.

"To be even minded is the greatest virtue."

-Heraclitus

2

"True rewards – wealth, knowledge, love, fitness, and equanimity – come from ignoring others and improving ourselves."

-Naval Ravikant

3.

"I begin to speak only when I'm certain what I'll say isn't better left unsaid."

-Cato

4.

"People hide their truest nature. I understood that; I even applauded it. What sort of world would it be if people bled all over the sidewalks, if they wept under trees, smacked whomever they despised, kissed strangers, revealed themselves."

-Alice Hoffman

5.

"He who fears death will never do anything worth of a man who is alive."

-Seneca

6.

"It's not what happens to you, but how you react to it that matters."

-Epictetus

7.

"To be calm is the highest achievement of the self."

-Zen Proverb

8.

"It never ceases to amaze me: we all love ourselves more than other people, but care more about their opinion than our own."

- Marcus Aurelius

9.

"With the new day comes new strength and new thoughts."

-Eleanor Roosevelt

10.

"Too many people believe that everything must be pleasurable in life."

-Robert Green

11.

"Time is like a river made up of the events which happen, and a violent stream; for as soon as a thing has been seen, it is carried away, and another comes in its place, and this will be carried away too."

-Marcus Aurelius

12.

"Self-control is strength. Right thought is mastery. Calmness is power."

-James Allen

13.

"Life begins at the end of your comfort zone."

-Neale Donald Walsch

14.

"If you lose self-control everything will fall."

-John Wooden

15.

"To be wronged is nothing unless you continue to remember it."

-Confucius

16.

"A single day among the learned lasts longer than the longest life of the ignorant."

-Posidonius

17.

"More is lost by indecision than wrong decision."

-Marcus Tullius Cicero

18.

"You can't force raging water to be calm. You have to leave it alone and let it return to its natural flow. Emotions are the same way."

-Thibaut

19.

"The obstacle is the way."

-Ryan Holiday

20.

"If anyone can refute me – show me I'm making a mistake or looking at things from the wrong perspective – I'll gladly change. It's the truth I'm after, and the truth never harmed anyone."

-Marcus Aurelius

21.

"Insight emerges out of silence."

-B. D. Schiers

22.

"No one saves us but ourselves. No one can and no one may. We ourselves must walk the path."

-Buddha

23.

"A fit body, a calm mind, a house full of love. These things cannot be bought – they must be earned."

-Naval Ravikant

24.

"Discomfort is the currency of success."

-Brooke Castillo

25.

"People tend to avoid the important work they fear by doing unimportant work that wears them out. They suppress anxiety with exhaustion, but they do not address the source of the problem."

-TheStoicEmperor

26.

"When you arise in the morning think of what a privilege it is to be alive, to think, to enjoy, to love."

-Marcus Aurelius

27.

"Once you know how to take care of yourself, company becomes an option."

-Keanu Reeves

28.

"Anything or anyone that angers you becomes your master."

-Epictetus

29.

"The wise man is neither raised up by prosperity nor cast down by adversity; for always he has striven to rely predominately on himself, and to derive all joy from himself."

-Seneca

30.

"Stoicism is about the domestication of emotions, not their elimination."

-Nassim Nicholas Taleb

31.

"If you haven't the strength to impose your own terms upon life, then you must accept the terms it offers you."

-T.S. Eliot

32.

"Everything we hear is an opinion, not fact. Everything we see is a perspective, not the truth."

-Marcus Aurelius

33.

"There is no better way to grow as a person than to do something you hate every day."

-David Goggins

34.

"Uncertainty is an uncomfortable position. But certainty is an absurd one."

-Voltaire

35.

"Empty your mind, be formless. Shapeless, like water. If you put water into a cup, it becomes the cup. You put water into a bottle and it becomes the bottle You put it in a teapot, it becomes the teapot. Now, water can flow or it can crash."

-Bruce Lee

36.

"Fall seven times, stand up eight."

-Japanese Proverb

37.

"In stillness lives wisdom. In quiet you'll find peace. In solitude you'll remember yourself."

-Robin Sharma

38.

"When we are unable to find tranquility within ourselves, it is useless to see it elsewhere."

-François de La Rochefoucauld

39.

"The best revenge is not to be like your enemy."

-Marcus Aurelius

40.

"You cannot hope to make progress in areas where you have made no application."

-Epictetus

41.

"This is our big mistake: to think we look forward to death. Most of death is already gone. Whatever time has passed is owned by death."

-Seneca

42

"Everything that happens to you is a form of instruction if you pay attention."

-Robert Greene

43.

"Now is the time to get serious about living your ideals. How long can you afford to put off who you really want to be? Your nobler self cannot wait any longer. Put your principles into practice – now."

-Epictetus

44.

"Difficulty is what wakes up the genius."

-Nassim Nicholas Taleb

45.

"Look back over the past, with its changing empires that rose and fell, and you can foresee the future too."

-Marcus Aurelius

46.

"The future belongs to those who prepare for it today."

-Malcolm X

47.

"Associate with people who are likely to improve you. Welcome those who you are capable of improving. The process is a mutual one: men learn as they teach."

-Seneca

48.

"Being attached to many things, we are weighed down and dragged by them."

-Marcus Aurelius

49.

"Problems only exist in the human mind."

-Anthony de Mello

50.

"It is not the mountain we conquer but ourselves."

-Edmund Hilary

51.

"If it is time to rest, rest completely. A good rest rejuvenates you so that you may do quality work. If it is time to work, work with complete focus. Time spent working earnestly earns you a well-deserved rest. Don't mix work and rest; this compromises the quality of both."

-TheAncientSage

52.

"Inwardly, we ought to be different in every respect, but outward dress should blend in with the crowd."

- Seneca

53.

"The impediment to action advances action. What stands in the way becomes the way."

-Marcus Aurelius

54.

"Without labor, nothing prospers."

-Sophocles

55.

"One loses joy and happiness in the attempt to possess them."

-Masanobu Fukuoka

56.

"No great thing is created suddenly, any more than a bunch of grapes or a fig. If you tell me that you desire a fig, I answer that there must be time. Let it first blossom, then bear fruit, then ripen."

-Epictetus

57.

"A gem cannot be polished without friction, nor a man perfected without trials."

-Seneca

58.

"Understand: people will constantly attack you in life. One of their main weapons will be to instill doubts about yourself. They will often disguise this as their objective opinion, but invariably it has a political purpose."

-Robert Greene

59.

"Your life will be in order when disorder ceases to bother you."

-James Pierce

60.

"Gratitude is not only the greatest of virtues, but the parent of all others."

-Marcus Tullius Cicero

61.

"The more tranquil a man becomes, the greater is his success, his influence, his power for good. The calmness of mind is one of the beautiful jewels of wisdom."

-James Allen

62.

"He has the most who is content with the least."

-Diogenes

63.

"You have power over your mind – not outside events. Realize this, and you will find strength."

- Marcus Aurelius

64.

"People are frugal in guarding their personal property; but as soon as it comes to squandering time they are most wasteful of the one thing in which it is right to be stingy."

-Seneca

65.

"Some can delay gratification. Others don't seek it at all. Be the latter."

-Maxime Lagacé

66.

"There is only one way to happiness and that is to cease worrying about things which are beyond the power of our will."

-Epictetus

67.

"Success is based off of your willingness to work your ass off no matter what obstacles are in your way."

-David Goggins

68.

"We are quick to forget that just being alive is an extraordinary piece of good luck, a remote event, a chance occurrence of monstrous proportions."

-Nassim Nicholas Taleb

69.

"The beginnings of all things are small."

-Ciccro

70.

"You are not tied to a particular position; your loyalty is not to a career or company."

-Robert Greene

71.

"A Stoic is someone who transforms fear into prudence, pain into transformation, mistakes into initiation, and desire into undertaking."

-Taleb Nassim Nicholas

72.

"A man is no bigger than the smallest thing that provokes him."

-Dan Horton

73.

"The ability to observe without evaluating is the highest form of intelligence."

-Jiddu Krishnamurti

74.

"Many will choose stability of slavery over the uncertainty of freedom."

-TheStoicEmperor

75.

"We should not, like sheep, follow the herd of creatures in front of us, making our way where others go, not where we ought to go."

-Seneca

76.

"When we are no longer able to change a situation, we are challenged to change ourselves."

-Viktor Frankl

77.

"What consumes your mind controls your life."

-Buddha

78.

"If anyone tell you that a certain person speaks ill of you, do not make excuses about what is said of you but answer, 'He was ignorant of my other faults, else he would have not mentioned these alone."

-Epictetus

79.

"Whatever happens at all happens as it should; you will find this true, if you watch narrowly."

-Marcus Aurelius

80.

"Remind yourself that the past and future are 'indifferent' to you, and the supreme good, and eudaimonia, can only exist within you, right now, in the present moment."

-Donald J. Robertson

81.

"The willing are led by fate, the reluctant dragged."

-Cleanthes

82.

"Bad companies are destroyed by crisis. Good companies survive them. Great individuals, like great companies, find a way to transform weakness into strength."

-Ryan Holiday

83.

"The most common act of violence is the relentless mental violence we perpetrate upon ourselves with nothing other than out thoughts."

-Bill Madden

84.

"Discomfort is a wise teacher."

-Caroline Myss

85.

"People should learn how to just be there, doing nothing."

-Thich Nhat Hanh

86.

"If you are pained by any external thing, it is not this thing that disturbs you, but your own judgement about it. And it is in your power to wipe out this judgement now."

- Marcus Aurelius

87.

"What we fear doing most is usually what we most need to do."

-Tim Ferris

88.

"People are always looking for shortcuts. The only way to achieve greatness in life is to have patience, consistency, and discipline."

-David Goggins

89.

"Give yourself fully to your endeavors. Decide to construct your character though excellent actions and determine to pay the price of a worthy goal. The trials you encounter will introduce you to your strengths."

-Epictetus

90.

"Difficulties strengthen the mind, as labor does the body."

-Seneca

91.

"How do you move forward? One step at a time. How do you lose weight? One kilo at a time. How do you write a book? One page at a time. How do you build a relationship? One day at a time. In a world obsessed with speed, never forget things of real worth and value take time."

-Thibaut

92.

"To complain is always non-acceptance of what is."

-Eckhart Tolle

93.

"Learn to detach yourself from the chaos of the battlefield."

-Robert Greene

94.

"Welcome if it comes. Let go if it goes. Chase nothing. Cling to nothing. Remain unconcerned."

-TheAncientSage

95.

"If it doesn't challenge you, it won't change you."

-Fred DeVito

96.

"Just that you do the right thing. The rest doesn't matter."

-Marcus Aurelius

97.

"We're never unhappy until we remember why we're supposed to be unhappy."

-Daniel V Chappell

98.

"Wealth consists not in having great possessions, but in having few wants."

-Epictetus

99.

"You never know how strong you are, until being strong is your only choice."

-Bob Marley

100.

"The only thing you can control is how you respond."

-Maxime Legacé

101.

"What you're supposed to do when you don't like a thing is change it. If you can't change it, change the way you think about it. Don't complain."

-Maya Angelou

102.

"Discipline is choosing between what you want now and what you want most."

-Abraham Lincoln

103.

"We suffer more often in imagination than in reality."

-Seneca

104.

"Freedom is the only worthy goal in life. It is won by disregarding thing that lie beyond our control."

-Epictetus

105.

"Be tolerant with others and strict with yourself."

-Marcus Aurelius

106.

"Sometimes in life we must fight not only without fear, but also without hope."

-Alessandro Pertini

107.

"Suffering arises from trying to control the uncontrollable."

-Epictetus

108.

"I don't mind what happens. That is the essence of inner freedom."

-Jiddu Krishnamurti

109.

"It's a sign of weakness to avoid showing signs of weakness."

-Nassim Nicholas Taleb

110.

"There is nothing more precious than trust. Low trust environments are full of friction and inefficiency. Every interaction is a fierce negotiation. Trust makes a marriage warm and a nation wealthy."

-TheStoicEmperor

111.

"The only real mistake is the one from which we learn nothing."

-Henry Ford

112.

"Reality is neutral. The world just reflects your own feelings back at you."

-Naval Ravikant

113.

"True happiness is to enjoy the present, without anxious dependence upon the future, not to amuse ourselves with either hope or fears but to rest satisfied with that we have, which is sufficient, for he that is so wants nothing."

-Seneca

114.

"If you chase two rabbits, you catch none."

-Confucius

115.

"Keep your intention pure. Emotions will try to distract you. So keep going. That's the cure."

-Maxime Lagacé

116.

"Heroes are heroes because they are heroic in behavior, not because they won or lost."

-Nassim Nicholas Taleb

117.

"Even the darkest night will end and the sun will rise."

-Victor Hugo

118.

"To be stoic is not to be emotionless, but to remain unaffected by your emotions."

-James Pierce

119.

"Having the fewest wants, I am nearest to the gods."

-Socrates

120.

"Short term thinking is everywhere. Noisy feuds over little prizes. The long term thinker will be king. Win the decade, not the day."

-TheStoicEmperor

121.

"Do not indulge in the dreams of having what you have not, but reckon up the chief of the blessings you do possess, and then thankfully remember how you would crave for them if they were not yours."

-Marcus Aurelius

122.

"Man conquers the world by conquering himself."

-Zeno of Citium

123.

"If a man knows not which port he sails, no wind is favorable."

-Seneca

124.

"What man actually needs is not a tensionless state, but rather the striving and struggling for some goal worthy of him."

-Viktor Frankl

125.

"You act like mortals in all that you fear, and like immortals in all that you desire."

-Seneca

126.

"How long are you going to wait before you demand the best for yourself?"

-Epictetus

127.

"Don't judge each day by the harvest you reap but by the seeds that you plant."

-Robert Louis Stevenson

128.

"Honesty is the first chapter in the book of wisdom."

-Thomas Jefferson

129.

"For many men, the acquisition of wealth does not end their troubles, it only changes them."

-Seneca

130.

"Compare yourself to who were yesterday, not to who someone else is today."

-Jordan Peterson

131.

"Complaining does not work as a strategy. We all have finite time and energy. Any time we spend whining is unlikely to help us achieve our goals. And it won't make us happier."

-Randy Pausch

132.

"Show people, don't tell people."

-David Goggins

133.

"He who laughs at the human race deserves better of it than he who mourns for it, for the former leaves it some good hopes of improvement, while the latter stupidly weeps over what he has given up all hopes of mending."

-Seneca

134.

"Weak men act to satisfy their needs, stronger men their duties."

-Nassim Nicholas Taleb

135.

"No human thing is of serious importance."

-Plato

136.

"Stay centered by accepting whatever happens to you. This is the ultimate."

-Chuang Tzu

137.

"You could leave right now. Let that determine what you do, say and think."

-Marcus Aurelius

138.

"Eventually, the time that was not spent on learning skills will catch up with you, and the fall will be painful."

-Robert Greene

139.

"Shallow men believe in luck. Strong men believe in cause and effect."

-Ralph Waldo Emerson

140.

"Until we have begun to go without them, we fail to realize how unnecessary many things are. We've been using them not because we needed them but because we had them."

-Seneca

141.

"Nowhere can man find a quitter or more untroubled retreat than in his own soul."

-Marcus Aurelius

142.

"Finding information is easier than ever. Filtering information is harder than ever. We are bombarded with irrelevant data and unsolicited stimulation. Choosing what to ignore is as important as choosing what to pay attention to"

-TheStoicEmperor

143.

"Treat every moment as your last. It is not preparation for something else."

-Shunryu Suzuki

144.

"The limit is not the sky. The limit is the mind."

-Wim Hof

145.

"A rational person can find peace by cultivating indifference to things outside of their control."

-Naval Ravikant

146.

"The best remedy for anger is delay."

-Seneca

147.

"Start living in discomfort. Gradually increase it little by little, and you will steadily grow. If you want sudden growth, deluge yourself in great discomfort and do not retreat from it."

-TheAncientSage

148.

"The ultimate power in life is to be completely self-reliant, completely yourself."

-Robert Greene

149.

"Don't seek for everything to happen as you wish it would, but rather that everything happens as it actually will – then your life will flow well."

-Epictetus

150.

"If you are depressed, you are living the past. If you are anxious, you are living in the future. If you are at peace, you are living in the present."

-Lao Tzu

151.

"The art of being wise is knowing what to overlook."

-William James

152.

"Give a man a fish, and you feed him for a day. Teach a man to fish, and you feed him for a lifetime."

-Unknown

153.

"Nothing endures but change."

-Heraclitus

154.

"Meditation is intermittent fasting for the mind. Too much sugar leads to a heavy body, and too many distractions lead to a heavy mind. Time spent undistracted and alone, in self-examination, journaling, meditation, resolves the unresolved and takes us from mentally fat to fit."

-Naval Ravikant

155.

"Waste no more time arguing what a good man should be. Be one."

-Marcus Aurelius

156.

"All know the way, but few actually walk it."

-Bodhidharma

157.

"It's your road and yours alone. Others may walk with it with you, but no one can walk it for you."

-Rumi

158.

"Order your soul. Reduce your wants."

-Augustine of Hippo

159.

"If you want others to be happy, practice compassion. If you want to be happy, practice compassion."

-14th Dalai Lama

160.

"We must indulge the mind and from time to time allow it the leisure which is its food and strength. We must go for walks out of doors, so that the mind can be strengthened by a clear sky and plenty of fresh air."

-Seneca

161.

"The universe only gives us what we think we're worthy of receiving."

-Joe Dispenza

162.

"Why should we pay so much attention to what the majority thinks?"

-Socrates

163.

"You don't develop courage by being happy in your relationships every day. You develop it by surviving difficult times and challenging adversity."

-Epicurus

164.

"The true hero is one who conquers his own anger and hatred."

-Dalai Lama

165.

Don't be the person that looks at the weather report the night before to decide what you are going to do the next day."

-David Goggins

166.

"True stoics don't care about the outcome. They just care to give their best shot, right here, right now."

-Maxime Lagacé

167.

"It is not the man who has too little, but the man who craves more, that is poor."

-Seneca

168.

"When you keep the peace with yourself, you also bring peace to others."

-Rhonda Byrne

169.

"Growth and comfort do not co-exist."

-Ginni Rometty

170.

"Comfort makes you weaker. We need some variability, some stressors. Not too much, but just enough."

-Nassim Nicholas Taleb

171.

"The meaning of life is just to be alive. It is so plain and so obvious and so simple. And yet, everybody rushes around in a great panic as if it were necessary to achieve something beyond themselves."

-Alan Watts

172.

"Never let people who choose the path of least resistance steer you away from your chosen path of most resistance."

-David Goggins

113.

"Only time can heal what reason cannot."

-Seneca

114.

"The truth is that our finest moments are most likely to occur when we are feeling deeply uncomfortable, unhappy, or fulfilled. For it is only in such moments, propelled by discomfort, that we are likely to step out of our ruts and start searching for different ways or truer answers."

-M. Scott Peck

115.

"The reason why we have two ears and only one mouth is so we might listen more and talk less."

-Zeno of Citium

116.

"Life is a storm that will test you unceasingly. Don't wait for calm waters that may not arrive. Derive purpose from resilience. Learn to sail the raging sea."

-TheStoicEmperor

117.

"Remember that very little is needed to make a happy life."

-Marcus Aurelius

178.

"It is impossible for a man to learn what he thinks he already knows."

-Epictetus

179.

"The mind should not be kept continuously at the same pitch of concentration, but given amusing diversions… Our minds must relax: they will rise better and keener after a rest."

-Seneca

180.

"Resisting life causes suffering. The cassation of suffering is letting go of holding on to ourselves."

-Pema Chodron

181.

"Some of the best things that have ever happened to us wouldn't have happened to us, if it weren't for some of the worst things that have ever happened to us."

-Mokokoma Mokhonoana

182.
"Some of us think holding on makes us strong; but sometimes it is letting go."

-Herman Hesse

183.
"Yesterday is not ours to recover, but tomorrow is ours to win or lose."

-Lyndon B. Johnson

184.
"Make the mind tougher by exposing it to adversity."

-Robert Greene

185.
"I do what is mine is to do, the rest does not disturb me."

-Marcus Aurelius

186.
"Stoicism, understood properly, is a cure for disease. The disease in question is the anxiety, grief, fear, and various other negative emotions that plague humans and prevent them from experiencing a joyful existence."

-William B. Irvine

187.

"Most of us attempt to avoid problems. This tendency is the primary basis of all human mental illness."

-Scott Peck

188.

"Don't seek to have events happen as you wish, but wish them to happen as they do happen, and all will be well with you."

-Epictetus

189.

"We must take a higher view of all things, and bear with them more easily: it better becomes a man to scoff at life than to lament over it."

-Seneca

190.

"Understand: in life as in war, nothing ever happens just as you expect it to."

-Robert Greene

191.

"Assume life will be really tough, and then ask if you can handle it. If the answer is yes, you've won."

-Charlie Munger

192.

"The meaning of life is to find your gift. The purpose of life is give it away."

-Pablo Picasso

193.

"These mountains that you are carrying, you were only meant to climb."

-Najwa Zebian

194.

"If you want happiness for an hour, take a nap. If you want happiness for a day, go fishing. If you want happiness for a month, get married. If you want happiness for a year, inherit a fortune. If you want happiness for a lifetime, help somebody else."

-Chinese Proverb

195.

"Be patient and tough; someday this pain will be useful to you."

-Ovid

196.

"All things are difficult before they are easy."

-Thomas Fuller

197.

"Death smiles at us all, but all a man can do is smile back."

-Marcus Aurelius

198.

"For your part, do not desire to be a general, or a senator, or a consul, but to be free; and the only way to this is a disregard of things which lie not within our own power."

-Epictetus

199.

"Everything can be taken from a man but one thing: the last of the human freedoms – to choose one's attitude in any given set of circumstances, to choose one's own way."

-Viktor Frankl

200.

"It's not that we have little time, but more that we waste a good deal of it."

-Seneca

201.

"It's part of being human to feel discomfort. We don't even have to call it suffering."

-Pema Chodron

202
"He who has a why to live can bear almost any how."

-Friedrich Nietzsche

203.
"What is to give light must endure burning."

-Viktor Frankl

204.
"Every hour focus you mind attentively… on the performance of the task in hand, with dignity, human sympathy, benevolence and freedom, and leave aside all other thoughts. You will achieve this, if you perform each action as if it were your last."

-Marcus Aurelius

205.
"Fear is a natural reaction to moving closer to the truth."

-Pema Chodron

206.
"True security lies in the unrestrained embrace of insecurity – in the recognition that we never really stand on solid ground, and never can."

-Oliver Burkeman

207.
"Move toward resistance and pain."

-Robert Greene

208.

"If you accomplish something good with hard work, the labor passes quickly, but the good endures; if you do something shameful in pursuit of pleasure, the pleasure passes quickly, but the shame endures."

-Gaius Musonius Rufus

209.

"A gift consists not in what is done or given, but in the intention of the giver or doer."

-Seneca

210.

"Your mind wants control. Life wants change."

-Maxime Lagacé

211.

"Discipline is the basic set of tools we require to solve life's problems. Without discipline we can solve nothing. With only some discipline we can solve only some problems. With total discipline we can solve all problems."

-Scott Peck

212.

"In every situation, life is asking us a question, and our actions are the answer."

-Ryan Holiday

213.

"Think of yourself as dead. You have lived your life. Now, take what's left and live it properly. What doesn't transmit light creates its own darkness."

-Marcus Aurelius

214.

"Don't just sit there. Do something. The answers will follow."

-Mark Manson

215.

"If you want to improve, be content to be thought foolish and stupid."

-Epictetus

216.

"There is nothing noble in being superior to your fellow man; true nobility is being superior to your former self."

-Ernest Hemingway

217.

"Be a master of the mind, not mastered by the mind."

-Zen Proverb

218.

"You are scared of dying – and, tell me, is the kind of life you lead really any different than being dead?"

-Seneca

219.

"Act without expectation."

-Lao Tzu

220.

"Desire is a contract that you make with yourself to be unhappy until you get what you want."

-Naval Ravikant

221.

"You need patience, discipline, and an agility to take losses and adversity without going crazy."

-Charlie Munger

222.

"Unfollow the mind. Follow the heart. Mute the masses."

-TheAncientSage

223.

"Sleep is the best meditation."

-14ᵗʰ Dalai Lama

224.

"Better to endure pain in an honorable manner than to seek joy in a shameful one."

-Massimo Pigliucci

225.

"There is no beginning and there is no end time. There is only your perception of time."

-Zen Proverb

226.

"Nothing that you have not given away will ever be really yours."

-C. S. Lewis

227.

"For beautiful eyes, look for the good in others; for beautiful lips, speak only words of kindness; and for poise, walk with the knowledge that you are not alone."

-Audrey Hepburn

228.

"Better to light one candle than to curse the darkness."

-Chinese Proverb

229.

"Never give up on a dream just because of the time it will take to accomplish it. The time will pass anyway."

-Earl Nightingale

230.

"Whatever you do in life, surround yourself with smart people who'll argue with you."

-John Wooden

231.

"Never interrupt someone doing what you said couldn't be done."

-Amelia Earhart

232.

"Wherever there is a human being, there is an opportunity for kindness."

-Seneca

233.

"Adopt the pace of nature: her secret is patience."

-Ralph Waldo Emerson

234.
"The more you care, the stronger you can be."

-Jim Rohn

235.
"The only true wisdom is in knowing you know nothing."

-Socrates

236.
"When someone is properly grounded in life, they shouldn't have look outside themselves for approval."

-Epictetus

237.
"In dwelling, live close to the ground. In thinking, keep to the simple. In conflict, be fair and generous. In governing, don't try to control. In work, do what you enjoy. In family life, be completely present."

-Lao Tzu

238.
"Turn your wounds into wisdom."

-Oprah Winfrey

239.

"If you don't know where you are going, any road will get you there."

-Lewis Carroll

240.

"The journey of a thousand miles begins with one step."

-Lao Tzu

241.

"Don't let schooling interfere with you education."

-Mark Twain

242.

"Between stimulus and response, there is a space. In that space is our power to choose our response."

-Viktor Frankl

243.

"He who reign within himself, and rules passions, desires, and fears, is more than a king."

-John Milton

244.

"What the superior man seeks is in himself; what the ordinary man seeks is in others."

-Confucius

245.

"There is no gain without struggle."

-Martin Luther King Jr

246.

"What upsets people is not things themselves, but their judgements about these things."

-Epictetus

247.

"It does not matter what you bear, but how you bear it."

-Seneca

248.

"If a man does not keep pace with his companions, perhaps it is because he hears a different drummer. Let him step to the music which he hears, however measured or far away."

-Henry David Thoreau

249.

"Life is not about finding yourself. Life is about creating yourself."

-George Bernard Shaw

250.

"Wherever you are, be totally there."

-Eckhart Tolle

251.

"Why do I keep repeating harmful behaviors/habits when I know they are bad for me? Because they give you pleasure or help you avoid discomfort. And you are too weak to let go of a little pleasure or to bear a little discomfort."

-TheAncientSage

252.

"Keep company only with those who uplift you."

-Epictetus

253.

"The secret of all victory lies in the organization of the non-obvious."

-Marcus Aurelius

254.

"The only thing you can control is the thought you are having right now. Make it calm, clear and simple."

-Maxime Lagacé

255.

"Live your life like you're the hero in your movie."

-Joe Rogan

256.

"As each day arises, welcome it as the very best day of all, and make it your own possession."

-Seneca

257.

"Expect the river to be wild, surprising and challenging. To expect the opposite is to live in delusion."

-Maxime Lagacé

258.

"Be so busy building your own life that other people's bullshit is of no concern."

-Ed Latimore

259.

"If it's endurable, then endure it. Stop complaining."

-Marcus Aurelius

260.

"If you want to know what a man's like, take a good look at how he treats his inferiors, not his equals."

-J. K. Rowling

261.

"Thinking is difficult, that's why most people judge."

-Carl Jung

262.

"Every experience is a lesson. Every loss is a gain."

-Sathya Sai Baba

263.

"He who knows all the answers has not been asked all the questions."

-Confucius

264.

"Don't do any task in order to get it over with. Resolve to do each job in a relaxed way, with all your attention. Enjoy and be one with your work."

-Thich Nhat Hanh

265.

"We are what we repeatedly do. Excellence, therefore. is not an act, but a habit."

-Will Durrant

266.

"You will earn the respect of all if you being by earning the respect of yourself."

-Gauis Musonius Rufus

267.

"Do you have the patience to wait until your mud settles and the water is clear?"

-Lao Tzu

268.

"Be silent or let thy words be worth more than silence."

-Pythagoras

269.

"Don't explain your philosophy. Embody it."

-Epictetus

270.

"Be rational, not emotional. Be proactive, not reactive. Have direction, not speed. Go slow. Choose Wisely."

-Maxime Lagacé

271.

"Remain calm in every situation because peace equals power."

-Joyce Meyer

272.

"It is not so much our friends' help that helps us as the confident knowledge that they will help us."

-Epicurus

273.

"If you only walk on sunny days, you'll never reach you destination."

-Paulo Coelho

274.

"The nearer a man comes to a calm mind, the closer he is to strength."

-Marcus Aurelius

275.

"Be present above all else."

-Naval Ravikant

276.

"I'm happy as hell, but I'm also real. Happy didn't get me here. But going through hell to get where I'm at made me happy."

-David Goggins

277.

"Learn to be indifferent to what makes no difference."

-Marcus Aurelius

278.

"Self-control is the chief element in self-respect, and self-respect is the chief element in courage."

-Thucydides

279.

"Begin at once to live, and count each separate day as a separate life."

-Seneca

280.

"One day, in retrospect, the years of struggle will strike you as the most beautiful."

-Sigmund Freud

281.

"Just keep in mind: the more we value things outside our control, the less control we have."

-Epictetus

282.

"The more time you spend in in your discomfort zone, the more your comfort zone will expand."

-Robin Sharma

283.

"It does not matter how slowly you go as long as you do not stop."

-Confucius

284.

"Conversation enriches the understanding, but solitude is the school of genius."

-Edward Gibbon

285.

"Don't argue with people nor insist on showing them truth. Maybe it is you who needs to change your mind. Even if you are right you only incur resentment by trying to correct others."

-TheAncientSage

286.

"Failure and deprivation are the best educators and purifiers."

-Albert Einstein

287.

"The search for happiness is one of the chief sources of unhappiness."

-Eric Hoffer

288.

"Stop drifting... Sprint to the finish. Write off your hopes, and if your well-being matters to you, be your own savior while you can."

-Marcus Aurelius

289.

"Think long term. Execute short term. Experience now."

-TheStoicEmperor

290.

"When you are trying to impress someone with words, the more you say, the more common you appear, and the less in control. Powerful people impress and intimidate by saying less. The more you say, the more likely you are to say something foolish."

-Robert Greene

291.

"The whole future lies in uncertainty: live immediately."

-Seneca

292

"In your actions, don't procrastinate. In your conversations, don't confuse. In your thoughts, don't wander. In your soul, don't be passive or aggressive. In your life, don't be all about business."

-Marcus Aurelius

293.

"Live intensely, live totally, here and now. Paradise is not some place, somewhere. It is a peace within you."

-Osho

294.

"When talent is lacking, habit will often suffice."

-James Clear

295.

"The things you think about determine the quality of your mind."

-Marcus Aurelius

296.

"If you cannot change something, it is best to accept it cheerfully rather than adding to ones misfortune by grieving over it."

-TheAncientSage

297.

"Opportunities multiply as they are seized."

-Sun Tzu

298.

"While we wait for life, life passes."

-Seneca

299.

"You will become what you give your attention to... If you yourself don't choose what thoughts and images you expose yourself to, someone else will."

-Epictetus

300.

"Progress is not achieved by luck or accident, but by working on yourself daily."

-Epictetus

301.

"By failing to prepare, you are preparing to fail."

-Benjamin Franklin

302.

"Cultivating of the mind is as necessary as food to the body."

-Marcus Tullius Cicero

303.

"You find peace by coming to terms with what you don't know."

-Nassim Nicholas Taleb

304.

"The difference between success and failure is the ability to take action."

-Alexander Graham Bell

305.

"They lose the day in expectation of the night, and the night in fear of the dawn."

-Seneca

306.

"Two things define you: Your patience when you have nothing and your attitude when you have everything."

-George Bernard Shaw

307.

"No amount of anxiety makes any difference to anything that is going to happen."

-Alan Watts

308.

"There are dark shadows on the earth, but its lights are stronger in the contrast."

-Charles Dickens

309.

"Freedom is not achieved by satisfying desire, but by eliminating it."

-Epictetus

310.

"I am not ashamed to confess that I am ignorant of what I do not know."

-Marcus Tullius Cicero

311.

"If you want something new, you have to stop doing something old."

-Peter Drucker

312.

"He who suffers before it is necessary, suffers more than is necessary."

-Seneca

313.

"Knowing yourself is the beginning of all wisdom."

-Aristotle

314.

"Worrying is like a paying a debt you don't owe."

-Mark Twain

315.

"True ignorance is not the absence of knowledge, but the refusal to acquire it."

-Karl Popper

316.

"Seek not the good in external things; seek it in yourselves."

-Epictetus

317.

"When you are upset you are likely to sacrifice the wellbeing of tomorrow to appease the hurt feelings of today. Not a good trade. Subject your emotions to a cooling off period before you allow them to guide major decisions."

-TheStoicEmperor

318.

"Judge a man by his questions rather than by his answers."

-Voltaire

319.

"What matters most is not what our obstacles are but how we see them, how we react to them, and whether we keep our composure."

-Ryan Holiday

320.

"Nothing is more honorable than a grateful heart."

-Seneca

321.

"If opportunity doesn't knock, build a door."

-Milton Berle

322

"He who angers you conquers you."

-Elizabeth Kenny

323.

"Being entirely honest with oneself is a good exercise."

-Sigmund Freud

324.

"Talk, but rarely, if occasion calls you, but do not talk of ordinary things – of gladiators or horse races or athletes or of meats or drinks – these are topics that arise everywhere – but above all do not talk about men in blame or compliment or comparison."

-Epictetus

325.

"I thought loving solitude was bad until I discovered a whole new world in it."

-Maxime Lagacé

326.

"What difference does it make, after all, what your position in life is if you dislike it yourself."

-Seneca

327.

"When it is obvious that the goals cannot be reached, don't adjust the goals, adjust the action steps."

-Confucius

328.

"Be silent for the most part, or, if you speak, say only what is necessary and in a few words."

-Epictetus

329.

"Self-discipline and self-control determine the quality of your life more than anything else."

-Ed Latimore

330.

"Life is not a matter of holding good cards, but of playing a poor hand well."

-Jack London

331.

"He who laugh at himself never runs out of things to laugh at."

-Epictetus

332.

"Never interrupt your enemy when he is making a mistake."

-Napoleon Bonaparte

333.

"Self-control is all about moment to moment self-awareness. You catch yourself doing – or about to do – something undesirable, see that it isn't good for you in the long term, and as a result of this awareness abstain from doing it."

-TheAncientSage

334.

"An investment in knowledge pays the best interest."

-Benjamin Franklin

335.

"If change is forced upon you, you must resist the temptation to overreact or feel sorry for yourself."

-Robert Greene

336.

"Settle on the type of person you want to be and stick to it, whether alone or in company."

-Marcus Aurelius

337.

"The pessimist complains about the wind; the optimist expects it to change; the realist adjusts the sails."

-William Arthur Ward

338.

"True happiness is to enjoy the present, without anxious dependence on the future."

-Seneca

339.

"When written in Chinese, the word 'crisis' is composed of two characters. One represents danger and the other represents opportunity."

-John F. Kennedy

340.

"Intelligence is the ability to adapt to change."

-Stephen Hawking

341.

"Other people's views and troubles can be contagious. Don't sabotage yourself by unwittingly adopting negative, unproductive attitudes through your association with others."

-Epictetus

342

"I live by letting things happen."

-Dogen

343.

"There are two ways of exerting one's strength: one is pushing down, the other is pulling up."

-Booker T. Washington

344.

"Forget the years, forget distractions. Leap into the boundless and make it your home."

-Zhuangzi

345.

"Failure is the opportunity to begin again, only more intelligently."

-Henry Ford

346.

"Do not try to seem wise to others."

-Epictetus

347.

"A happy life consists in tranquility of the mind."

-Marcus Tullius Cicero

348.

"Life is truly known only to those who suffer, lose, endure adversity and stumble from defeat to defeat."

-Anais Nin

349.

"Those who do not move, do not notice their chains."

-Rosa Luxemburg

350.

"Believe you can and you're half way there."

-Theodore Roosevelt

351.

"The soul becomes dyed with the color of its thoughts."

-Marcus Aurelius

352.

"Life can only be understood backwards; but it must be lived forwards."

-Soren Kierkegaard

353.

"Curiosity is the seed of knowledge."

-Francis Bacon

354.

"It is better to conquer our grief than to deceive it."

-Seneca

355.

"If you seek tranquility, do less."

-Marcus Aurelius

356.

"One must be gullible yet skeptical, sane yet mad, proud yet humble, warm yet indifferent, faithful yet a heretic, loving yet uncompromising, fearless yet cautious, open yet decisive. These are not contradictions. They make a person whole. And above all one must be whole, not fragmentary."

-TheAncientSage

357.

"Silence is a source of great strength."

-Lao Tzu

358.

"He is a wise man who does not grieve for the things which he has not, but rejoices for those which he has."

-Epictetus

359.

"Fools give up fast. Strong men persevere. The wise keep going forever."

-Maxime Lagacé

360.

"True bravery is doing what is right even when it's not popular."

-David Roads

361.

"Practice even what seems impossible."

-Marcus Aurelius

362.

"Be careful whom you associate with. It is human to imitate the habits of those with whom we interact. We inadvertently adopt their interests, their opinions, their values, and their habit of interpreting events."

-Epictetus

363.

"Set your heart on your work but never on its reward."

-Vyasa

364.

"No loss should be more regrettable to us than losing our time, for it is irretrievable."

-Zeno of Citium

365.

"Let us not postpone anything, let us engage in combats with life each day."

-Seneca

Epilogue

We live in a chaotic world that is frequently evolving. Despite any negative circumstances that may surround us, we must understand that it is our thoughts that dictate our state, not external occurrences. While we may not always have control over the events affecting us, we can however, maintain control in how we react to any given circumstance.

Emperors, artists, writers, entrepreneurs, and many more throughout history have practiced Stoicism in search of clarity, happiness, virtue, and resilience. No matter where you are in life, quotes from those whose wisdom has stood the test of time can serve as a challenging outlook and help to solve the problems of life.

I hope these quotes have helped strengthenen your perspective, and broadened your way of thinking. I wish you all the best as you continue on your pursuit of self-mastery.

If you liked this book, it would be sincerely appreciated if you could leave a review on Amazon. Let me know what you liked or even what you didn't like, as it helps me release better books in the future.

-Tate Harris

CPSIA information can be obtained
at www.ICGtesting.com
Printed in the USA
LVHW081411040421
683394LV00010B/1527